TO NO ONE BUT A FEELING.

E.A.MAY

SECOND EDITION.

ISBN: 979-8-9946238-0-0

TRIGGER WARNING:

THE FOLLOWING POETRY HAS VERY SENSITIVE SUBJECT MATTER(S) AND MAY BE TRIGGERING FOR SOME. PLEASE BE CAUTIOUS OF THE CONTENT, AND PLEASE READ WITH GRACE.

TO NO ONE BUT A FEELING

We are pages to a story longer than anticipated.

To no one but a feeling, it was only a feeling.

TO NO ONE BUT A FEELING

11/25/2023

Viña Del Mar / Chile

Open your heart, see what happens.

Maybe the flowers don't bloom the same on this side. Maybe the glass isn't as foggy as before. Cars aren't parked on the same side of the street, the traffic lights are different here.

Change courses and love differently.

Maybe you've been missing something.

ARGENTINA.

12/07/2023 1:26 AM

To no one but a feeling.

Remember the next time you love someone, remember laying down beside them.

If you want to love them. If you want to know what's next and what real effort looks like:

Remember you also deserve kindness and that you don't need to sabotage it in order to feel it finally pressed against your skin.

Accept it in any form it comes in.
Embrace it and hold it with open arms.

Love so deep that even in strange circumstances can come out with peace.

The roughest waters can be clear and soft when they crash.

Remember the feeling of how it could feel, loving someone unconditionally, wholeheartedly, and all at once.

I learned how much she cares

The long pauses in between stares and the oblivion underneath our eyelids

I hope she tells me something I never thought about

Swallowing rawness leaves a bad taste in her mouth
She wishes to be understood just like everyone else
Calm and collected but loud and not obnoxious

I sit here wondering if she'll ever feel lips pressed against her without sharp edges that cut like razor blades

I've watched her cry one too many times

The first time it cuts deep, then they're suddenly paper cuts, you look at for two seconds and wipe off with ease

Let it bleed, let it dry, tomorrow it will be fine

Let yourself be moved by anyone and everything.

Pink flowers in wine bottles, please tell me something I don't know.

The more hurt hovers over you.

The more you think there's a chance to fix their pain, the more we push and begin to understand the depth of how sitting in their silence with them... it all finally makes sense.

Do you think love is supposed to be one-dimensional?

Or do we all wish to accept it that way, so we don't run from it…

Elephants trumpet rooms like they need to claim them as their own, but the silence is deafening.

So loud… that I can feel their trunks whispering in my ears.

Conversations lead to intimacy, but another kind of intimacy.

Hands gripped and soft touches, but no sexual urgency wishes to be performed.

Change your appearance

Look smarter
Look harder
Look older
Look bolder

Be bolder
Be free

I want to know about your intimacy
How you show it and allow it to break

We must hurt to find an embrace

I sit here in silence, trying to replace

No,

Retrace

Retrace skin so elegantly
Let me fall where your veins begin and end

Let them lead me to your heart and back to your ring finger

I want to remember details that can't be erased

I always ruin it when it gets good
I always ruin it when it gets hard

Please don't run away…
But if you have to, I'll let you go

Maybe you'll come back tomorrow, or pick up the phone

Please pick up the phone.

ARGENTINA
DECEMBER 2023

Why can I sit here
And feel the energy shifting

How everyone walks
How the florists speaks to me

What the man who gave me bread this morning was thinking

Why can I sit here
and absorb…

I never liked taking.

12/13/2023 0009
LOS ANGELES

I want something that's hard. I want the world to allow me to love hard things. The hard things that are easy for not a handful of people.

Show me corners of the world that only I know I can reach.

BACK HOME
VENTURA COUNTY
12/18/2023
3:13

I'm scared

I'm scared they're going to wake up one day and realize that they need to be with someone who doesn't bring them peace, maybe someone who can build a white picket fence

I'm scared you'll leave because I leave people

I'm scared of all the karma I have yet to receive

All the time

I'm not a person who can stay for too long
Or maybe I can, but I never gave myself the opportunity to stay because I feel like I don't deserve it

I'll leave and pretend that it was the best option for you instead of myself

And I don't know why I run away

I don't understand why I can't sit in uncomfortableness and hardship for too long

Even though I met it and stayed with it for almost a full quarter of my life

I don't want to be its friend sometimes

I still run

And I don't want to run anymore.

Maybe lips have
the ability to
correct all the people
who misgendered me years ago.

I wish you weren't
the cure but sometimes
we all need that person to
open our eyes.

I want to go back to the day we were little kids

I wish I grew up on Calvert St instead of Ventura Blvd

Maybe if I knew you when we were kids our bodies wouldn't have had so much oxygen ripped out of us early

Maybe we would hold hands and play Tedder ball together

We would've had bloody knees and scabbed hands

But I don't actually wish that

Because in this universe and every other one, I lay beside you

We look at family photographs and laugh

You tell me the sky is gray today and I'll tell you it will be blue tomorrow

I sit on your living room floor with your dog and you sleep on the couch

I'll tell you to calm down and you'll tell me to get home safe

I always wanted a sister and I'm so glad I finally have one

It's raining and
the droplets are
getting heavier.

They remind me of hard times.

Cause even when
the earth is sad,
it cries too.

So, under jokes and laughter, when we want to stop breathing.

The oxygen we once
thought we were losing
became our friends' words.

Family was about blood for so long.

Once it sheds, we realize all the harm it causes.

You began building houses with people who were cut from the same cloth.

People who carry three times the weight of most, but we carry it so well that it barely looks like 5 kilos.

Our backs curve.

Don't look down on those who don't sit up straight.

Men want you with an
ellipsis, not a period.

For them, everything
continues after you…

And for you, everything
ends after them.

Do you want to fall in love
or pass the time you have left?

Sit at a coffee shop

They're in front of me

Maybe you'll look at me differently when I tell you how you should give yourself more credit than you deserve

Sit tight and be scared

The love I dream about might be in a stranger

Or in a friend

I'm willing to wait, but sometimes it gets lonely

Then I'm in a contradiction because I love my space and serenity

And then I drink my coffee and look around in peace…

I stop giving attention to negative things

Now I let someone cut me off on the freeway and turn my music up

Now I sit inside of patience when someone makes me upset

I will not hate you for who you are
But if you hate yourself, I will not carry that around with me

I worked too hard to build myself

I will not let you storm into my skin because you feel like committing murder

Do you
want to
fall in love
with me?

Sorry. Sometimes I say things that I don't mean. Sometimes yes, I do not think about certain things. My mind races, but it stops at times. Maybe it starts feeling bad for me and all it puts me through. I'm built with mistakes. It started when I was conceived. I was half wanted but then I was needed. At every single moment. I'm quite exhausting, I don't think I've ever fully rested in my entire life. I've built so many houses and had to leave them because I wasn't wanted in there anymore. I used to take it personally, but I realized that love isn't conditional at all. I want to give my all, all the time; it becomes too intense to consume; it's almost like I'm always begging, pleading, and yearning. I really hope you understand that one day. I know I'm not for everyone, so I found peace with being alone all the time. Actually, this has always been what I did. I don't think my emotions were ever safe until I finally talked to a therapist for the first time. Sometimes I wish I processed things better, but I don't think my nervous system likes that. I'm very loved and I think that's why I feel loving so easily. I recycle it.

I hope my person
loves animals; I hope
their heart aches
for their unconditional love.

Raw intuition.

There are so many layers to life
So many layers of empathy

The surface is only touched slightly when you haven't sat at fast food restaurants as a luxury

You didn't need to keep tags on your clothes

You didn't have to use the same toothbrush for years

The small things your mom would do so you wouldn't notice that her bank account reached one cent

Maybe you've gone through other things

But the layers have weight to them

And as much as you carry things easily, not all of us carry the same weight, so let's be gentle.

Even if I'm not on your mind, I still want to be an option and hopefully a choice.

I spent too long building up who I am just to have someone come in and try to break me down.

How can a person know so much information?

I thought I was the only one that could decipher humans in their own element

How arrogant of me, to never have a chance to devour that

I guess when you grow up knowing who's footsteps are going up the stairs you realize the love they could truly give

But you would've destroyed yourself for me

You would have done everything

And that's not love

Because why would I allow you to kill yourself in front of me

Allow people to love you for who you are

What’s the worst that can happen?

Doors are meant to open and close.

Am I always going to feel the heartbreak of when I found out?

Will the phone ring to nothing every time I tried calling you.

She cares

Maybe a little too much

Maybe she wishes she didn't care so much

but who else is going to go to protests and shout to people
who else cooks for you when you're feeling down

who else will be your shelter?

Although it is pure, kind, and innocent

we wish we were treated in the same essence but in this lifetime, we cannot ask for what we give

We are the healers of this world and that's all there is

When I write about people
I imagine them in a coffee shop
or sitting in front of me in a room filled
with quiet whispers and loud typing

But I soon realize that it only happens
when I think of you in silence, across from
each other, and only random laughter fills the
space around us

If I could spend the rest of my life in
coffee shops sitting in silence with you I
would

Sometimes I sit and think about how much
family I have, and I realize

My family stretches far from its roots and
genetics

You're my family, and I'll sit in coffee
shops for the rest of my life with you,
regardless of the motive

I wrote expensive poetry under your name,
and you pulled it out like it was the last
penny in your account.

Soft touches and innocent fingertips.

What more could I ask for?

Something I never asked for.

When I love
When I want to love someone
I want you
I want all of you
The good
The bad
The in between

And I don't like who you are anymore

this wasn't about her, was it?

No.

It was about me the whole time.

I'm just so tired.

From drugged eyes that passed by to handholding in Paris

I sit here for the second time under the Eiffel Tower and realize all the unnecessary pain you've put me through

I don't want to share a bed with you anymore
I don't want to keep testing boundaries every time we're together
I'm tired of the hard breathing and the empty promises
I'm over the long looks and cruel undertones
Please leave my skin alone
Let me go so I can find someone that tells me they love me for who I am and admires it with their voice

The actions you've brought to the table at what cost

I hoped that maybe if I learned to love you, it could have been greater than all the hurt, but it wasn't, because it was never real, I never loved you
I hoped everything felt less like hell and more like heaven

But you know what you were doing since the beginning

Under red lights, please get off me
I hoped you stopped it from happening, but you never do until it's too late

Do you know when to quit?

Do you know when to stop?

I can't sleep when I'm with you because of the constant questions that keep me up at night

As I touch your back one last time, I realize that everything I ever felt for you had been completely ripped away from me when you decided to get in the car and let me go, you taught me that I can have love and not love you

There will never be another fire that wants me like yours but at least for the second time in my life I choose my peace, and I choose myself

So please leave me alone because this burns with unkind intentions

I cared about you enough.

I'm tired of making a fool of myself

I'm just so tired.

Let them go.

It isn't right to
keep them hostage
in your heart.

I'm tired of watching you trying to throw things off balance to see how you could come back to it later. Wondering if you've reached different results.

Pushing buttons, see if they still do what they're supposed to or if they changed magically overnight.

I've seen you in your rawest form
I've entered your home
I've seen your walls
I've seen the mess
The unfiltered mouthful of words
The kindness
The lack of entitlement
The actions behind your words

Collect a thought
Commit to it
I hope she's loved in this lifetime

I sit with my mouth closed every time you need someone to do things for you.

I can't force my kindness if you wish for validation.

Please come.

I hope you don't quiet the voices in my head.
I hope you know how to turn them off.

But it's not your job to turn off the radio when it gets too loud but it's still nice to know its loud for you too.

Where there was once innocence and white glances

She painted the room red

It divided everything into a different perspective,

Not knowing who you are

Confused people

I wanted you to want me so bad that I allowed you to touch me with dirty hands instead of ones that came home from work and remembered to clean up before touching me

My soul rejected you, and I'll always remember the week I felt sick to my stomach

I'm glad I left when I needed to
You always know when you need to

When you've had enough.

I strongly believe in showing up for the people who made you.

Warm up a towel when it's cold out

Cook breakfast or get them coffee when you sleep over

Fill up their fridge when its empty if they can't afford one more fruit for the week

Clean your dishes and there's because they've been stacked for a couple days and maybe they don't have the energy to do them

Listen
Learn

Stick to genuine times where you stay afloat beside them

Hoping everyone loves them like you do

Even in the dark they shine

Your eyes widen to see them so easily, why can't love, always crave to be this pure.

I enjoy your presence
I enjoy your soul

I like you as a person

Words we all wish to hear

What are you thinking about?

It's almost like the person knew the narrator was short of words.

Strobe lights and dark rooms
That's the first time I felt

But the next time crowds fall to the ground
and we're the only ones at eye level

I wish the best for you
I hope all the pain you've been through
carries you into someone's arms who truly
cares about you

That has the patience to unravel all the
pain

I hope they remind you that in this
lifetime, you can love and be loved

In between suicidal thoughts and intrusive predicaments.

I hope to find a kind, caring soul underneath all the pain and turmoil that this world puts us through.

Drunk nights.

Your body is speaking to me right now, but it's not giving me permission.

Wonder what makes you think you do?

Leave them alone. Your hands don't need to be wrapped around them.

I forgot you cover your mirrors.

Asshole.

A man who kisses and loves like a woman.

That's all I'll ever be.

She stays with me.

I'll never put her to sleep.

Our souls were lost, and we found each other, we learned, so thank you.

That didn’t mean we were meant to stay.

She has a gaslit fire under her
But it burns you with violence and rage. No caution tape. None at all.

Once I started listening even closer to people, I realized nothing's ever about me unless it's coming out of my mouth.

I was thinking of home in all the wrong ways…

I don't think anyone can be my home

But I wouldn't mind having someone to talk to in my front yard when I'm finished building it

Or someone that has a cup of coffee with me inside

That's all we'll ever need in order to become whole, truly

When friendships
become
your romance.

I want my patience back

Let me love enough with so much patience and energy that I don't feel sick to my stomach waking up in the morning to walk

No matter if two or eight hours were rested, I want to get up so I can be there for you even when my days aren't so bright

Because to love has always been inside me and I wish to always lead life in this manner

And if I ever turn around in bed and say no out of ungratefulness, please let me rest because the morning was too much, and I apologize for that.

Do similarities
mean you should be
together, or do they
mean you should be apart…

What's on your mind?

Someone I thought I only saw.

Please take care
of her with
open arms

She's scared
of those who
wish her harm

I hope venom doesn't sip into a crowded room while we're laughing with each other

I hope a friend's cold heart doesn't freeze us to death

I hope they see it and leave it alone

Because I know it hurts to see another being loved like you want to be

But that doesn't mean we can't watch everyone be happy to process our own grief

Because if I sat here in my lonesome and tried to bath in dirty water, I wouldn't be able to let go of another soul ever again

Love is detachment

Learn how to let go

She's not religious if you listened.

She is if you didn't.

I hope to find a love that’s like a fireplace.

I wouldn’t mind your arms wrapped around me for the rest of my life.

Allow me to get cold feet to remember how I can always warm them up. For when I’m with you, there’s a fire, and I’ll always stay warm by your side.

But everyone's love burns so far.

The way she entered my life could be a catalyst for something missing in it so easily.

Please put me down and let me go. I cannot be owned by anyone but myself.

Your possessiveness will push me away, and the lack of self-worth will control you in ways that continue to move you in oblivion.

Are we more worried
about why they lied
or should we ask why
they kept it from us?

I can like you and respect you at the same time.

My feelings for you shouldn't dictate the way I treat you as a person.

What a selfish act I will never conquer.

Skin.

I don't want it touched; I was under bodies that gripped too tightly.

I'm sorry, I was lost; I should've fought it better.

I've learned lessons through them…

They've all taught me things

They taught me how to be patient

How to love unconditionally

To make sure that in every situation we're against it, not against them

They taught me self-love

They taught me how to be family-oriented

They taught me so much

And now I get to make sure you're not another lesson

The next time I touch lips, I wish to bite them gently and not leave the taste of blood

When your memory fades away, I hope to be the one who has all of them safe.

So, when you regain your life even for a second, I can remind you of how bright you've always been, a friendly love I wish to embody.

Do you want to know what hurts a lot?

When you can feel your friends' hearts breaking while holding them.

Every bone in their body seems to be falling apart.

Vibrating with pain.

Their hearts beat faster.

The tears can't be held in anymore.

Sometimes we all just need a hug.

A hug so long that everything you've been keeping inside comes out.

The floor is your home for a few minutes as you catch your breath.

You can feel the veins draining while your hands hold onto their wrists.

We break in odd ways.

Crying so hard you grab onto them because that's the only way you can feel human.

Confidence doesn't come from a man who sits in a suit with glass windows surrounding him.

It's a woman who trusted a man for so long that moving out and moving into another stranger's house was too easy.

I must have done something right in my life to deserve so many people's love and appreciation

I must have done something right to deserve all the kind words and the laughter that consumes us all, the quiet rooms that only you can hear the noise

09/08/2023

Words for my future lover

She's near, I can feel it.

I don't plan to be different

I plan to move into your heart and call it my home

Let it grow.
Let it pass.
Let it fade.

Control. Control. Control.

No more.

This love story
isn't platonic or romantic.

It's intimate.

Put your heart on the line. Maybe they'll have your back. Maybe their veins are meant to pump your blood through them.

You'll just never know the truth, will you?

I'd rather have no money in my bank account because I gave it to someone who has less than me than to have money that I don't need.

The emotional turbulence you experience when just a country over, peace is not known at all.

Although guns run down our school hallways, the pain lies within ending human life for petty fights and small gains.

The number of bodies that need to be piled for one person to feel better about themselves.

To know peace at any moment in your life is to have privilege.

With the power you hold, remember the hurt, but don't drown in it.

If you disrespect people behind their backs, it doesn't create peace for your mind, it distinguishes your lack of love and sanity for yourself.

You'll never be the victim; you so desperately need to be.

When you're written by a woman, you hold the pain of a thousand of them before you.

So don't ask me if I agree with you as a man because the answer is no.

Until you know this pain, you will never understand.

I think I associate green with safety because my best friend's table in their dining room is that color. I love how the word home comes to mind as we all sit around and eat meals made from scratch.

When they drive you crazy and bring you peace.

That’s how you know you can love without limits.

Because why else would my brain care so much, and why must it take so much space in order to understand you?

The candle next to my dresser

The clean floors and the smell of freshness on my sheets

The words written on my walls

The pillow that's longer than me

The rays that sneak through my bedroom windows

The fresh water that I consume, and I let pour on my body

I don’t want to take someone’s clothes off

I want to just feel closer to them than I already do

I don’t think of a naked body as a tool for my pleasure, but as an art that I can trace with my fingers and slowly admire each pore

Let’s revisit.

She leaves doors open, but not all the way, just a small crack, so when she decides she wants something, she can sneak back in and get it without you noticing.

Like I said before. She holds love, but she doesn’t know what love is. So, she masks the ability of it but doesn’t fully extend her hand to hold you up when you’re down.

I wish it were different, that maybe you could be a home, but only one, I must leave at some point.

You will never be a sanctuary.

I think things are slipping and getting lost in translation

I want love in whatever form it needs to come in

But you're so scared to love that you can't even do that for yourself

I want to be touched, but by those who are here because I'm the person they want to touch

Not the person who is easy for them to touch

The true calling doesn't live here; the constant push and pull is going to eat me alive, regardless of where we stand

So please stop playing games and sit down

Because when I stop touching you

I'll never touch you again

Sorry for
your loss.

Hmm. You know words are supposed to mean so much more than they are, but for some reason, when there's a moment in time where there's loss and agony, we tend to always recycle words to make others feel better.

But words lose their meaning over time.

I'm sorry for your loss. No, how about:

I see your pain, and I'm here for you.

How about:

I want to be here for you.

And watch people, see how they show up.

I realized a long time ago how I hold
people.

I'll sit with you and hold you until your
panic calms down.

I'll hold your hand when you're crying your
eyes out in my passenger seat.

I'll kiss your forehead when your head is
against my chest.

I'll let you sleep in my arms and let my
arm fall asleep to your comfort.

I'm just a kid sitting on the bathroom
floor, seeing my mother cry for the first time
in 8 years.

And I don't think caring about people
should be so shallow.

Swallow your pride and love them no matter
what.

Love because you don't want anything.

Love to love.

There are so many
people who have
pieces of me.

That no one
else will
ever have.

I don't think I have the capability to fall in love.

But why is the word love not a word anymore, when will I allow it to be an action.

Or have I already found myself in it?

The mess you made.
Why do I know how to clean it up?

El desorden que dejastes.
Por qué sé cómo limpiarlo?

I don't want, easy.

Learn another language even if it takes years.

Learn about where they grew up, even if you need to walk ten miles each way to figure it out, figure it out.

Hear their voice crack when there's a mention of an uneasy emotion.

The sound of safety could bring people into each other's arms like we've been wearing headphones all along.

I don't want, easy.

I want it to be hard.

I don’t want
another body
imprinted on
my sheets,
only my own.

Respecting women came naturally. Respecting them came from the soul fact that I respected myself as a woman, and I still do. I visit her at times, so she can pull me back from the grips of misogyny.

She's done so much for me, and I can never repay her for the damage she didn't need to fix.

Even between loud music
I hope I can hear your heartbeat once you arrive

Even with enemies around
Your peace is where I'll drown

Hear the whispers
But you're the only sound

Thank you for not being different

A stranger who slams doors can hide in plain sight

But a man with good intentions will always find his peace even in the worst situations

Thank you for not being peaceful

Friends.

As he touched my skin.

The thought of no one else came to mind, but as soon as my eyes opened, I realized much more than I could bare.

Don't speak of being
friends
when
lovers
is on your mind.

I wonder if you still hate shoes on the bed, and if that was lost as well.

Words never came naturally with her.

My pages would read blank as I tried to force any feelings on a piece of paper.

It's really fucked up if you think about it for too long.

And I truly hope when it's time, they flow as naturally as the ocean clashes on the sand.

Spill love. Care more.

I thought I wasn’t meant to hold all this. I wonder where it ends, begins and where it meets.

Lips that cure the mind. Lips that read. Show me parts of myself where I can finally allow myself to write on paper for hours.

I lived with
a stranger for
almost four years.

She was naked at night, but she was never vulnerable.

Her cold heart collected all her thoughts, and she never warmed herself up enough to say them out loud.

I lived with
a stranger for
almost four years.

Each year had a limit on the number of words that we would exchange, and by the almost fourth year, nothing was left to be said.

I lived with
a stranger for
almost four years.

I'll accept the way you love
The shattered child
And the broken heart
Your emotional journey
The likelihood of your swing set of moods
I'll learn to hold space for the child who was knocked down and the one who stood up
The lingering feelings of the inevitable in your life
The yes
The no's
The need for space
The grip of your hands
The thought of martyrdom and rage
The crimes that come with loving you
I'll hold your body without taking your clothes off
I'll trace skin with graceful opportunity and no malus gripping
Even my hand around your throat will never leave a scar

I think about it, the things we didn't get to do.

And that's why I grieve so heavily,

Neck kiss.
No sexual thought.
Tender.
No Malus.

I want to feel someone's neck with my lips while I brush my teeth.

I want the silence around us to call, and I want to know you hold the strength to answer it.

If life gives me only one person to love, I will choose them and sleep with strangers just to pass the time.

Or maybe I'll sit in silence within myself.

You can't find a home in those who don't speak to your soul.

So please tell me, you're different.

Because you're not.

You're just like everyone else.

I understand the moments are here for now, not for later, not forever.

I want someone who
isn’t afraid to hurt me.

Because pain is meant to be felt.

It doesn’t
always mean
we’re suffering.

I like men, but unfortunately, no one can satisfy me like the love of someone who identifies as a woman.

I think about the fact that no matter how many voids I fill. How many people, I meet.

They're not me.

And I can sit in silence in a room with myself, and nothing else will feel like home.

Because my rib cages have always been my walls, especially when I would curve them inward.

So, I sit here with my hands drying paint and my other smearing it on words across a cardboard, and I don't think I realize that those are the happiest moments because I'm always so distracted with life.

I can’t even say I care about you in English. I feel like the words aren’t as powerful as the word “cariño” is in Spanish.

I could cry about it forever

And that's a long time for someone who doesn't drink water…

He wants to learn languages together.

He doesn't want to just sit around and create empty conversations about meaningless topics.

There's too much
love in this world
to be giving it to
just one person.

I find it beautiful when I randomly cry, lyrics puncture old wounds, or the reminder that you don't exist anymore hurts a little too much.

You've taught me to be human again.

Being in your arms again.

I can finally rest.

I'm so glad I get to be home again on your chest.

You know how people say to focus on the people who haven't left you.

Who still care, love, and show up?

I agree with that.

But what if the people died?

I sit here realizing that only a few know the heartaches that one has gone through and the transformation that they have undergone

The effect of those who love us unconditionally should never go unappreciated, for I have once felt alone in this world, and now I sit here and realize the only thing that kept me alone was myself and my fear of allowing people to know me and move into my life like waves

Because they aren't at fault for who they are

They are not at fault for how life works for them

They make choices, but sometimes we aren't their choices, and that's okay

We move on

We leave

Or sometimes we stay

And sometimes our paths cross again

But over time, you begin to realize not everyone is out to get you

You...

The answer is you were always out to get yourself.

Every time I see them

I picture myself sitting on the concrete floor and not being able have the strength to get up to hug them

I spent the whole way over crying

My eyes burned

I'm on my second cigarette

They have a smile on their face

They look over and sit next to me

And the silence gets louder as I slowly mouth the words "they found her body on the side of the road"

And the silence

There was actual silence.

So, I’ll get up every morning

I’ll try my best to breathe and live

Because maybe you wanted that

And you weren’t given that choice

I feel alone

I feel so isolated all the time

That's why I always push others' families onto me

Because I've never had one big enough to celebrate things with

It feels so lonely

I barely have them around

My mom is alive, so she made me feel alone or made me think I'm alone, so I only had her as a resource, and I'm tired of it, honestly

Everyone else gets to celebrate with their family and be around them, but I just feel so alone cause when I bring someone home, I'm not bringing them to a gathering with food and a dance party or a vacation, I'm bringing them to my mom, my dad and brother. That should be enough.

And yet, I prioritize friendship because that's what became my family, but even they have people

Even their parents, too, I prioritize them because they allow me to grow and not stay in four walls

I'm not lonely

Because to be lonely is to be weak

At least that's what my mother said

But why is it that her voice is in my head all the time instead of mine

I don't feel like a person 90% of the time

And when I get that 10% I can feel all my own emotions drowning me as I try to speak

I want you out

I want to carve everything out with a knife or with pills, so I can make sure I never come back to these thoughts

I'm tired of believing maybe this time, when I say I'm happy, you won't say "yeah, we'll see how long that lasts" because that crack you leave open happens to be the hole that starts to take everything away from me, and I don't want that to happen anymore

I don't want to lose her because you told me I wasn't enough to be loved

I don't want to love you the way I loved her

I know you'll mean so much more than that

I feel alone…

My mom built me a self-esteem; she made sure she was the only one who could knock it all down.

I think if you cheated on me, I would've been able to forgive you in a blink of an eye because at least I would know that you didn't care as comfort.

But the fact that I was at my lowest and you chose to defend your arrogance really made me see who you were all along.

My kid was going to grow up with those who touched you without your permission.

With people who hit, slapped, and didn't want to grow.

People who chose to live with a partner that could've changed but chose not to, so the only way was to keep them around, because being alone was harder than being reminded every day.

My mother had the privilege to get up and leave my father after the first time he raised his hands.

My mother raised me to stand up for myself, and I won't apologize for that anymore.

So, it makes sense why you chose to turn me into a monster, and I allowed myself to do so.

You longed for your father so badly that you needed to turn me into him, so you felt whole.

But I was never that.

But your pain turned into my pain so easily and I loved you so blindly.

So, stay quiet.
Stay quiet and don't talk about it.

Don't have the hard conversations.

Take it to your grave and make sure no one reads both sides of the story on your tomb stone.

I'll still bring you flowers.

And as
the pieces

fall from your statue,

I know I’ll always be there
to hold them in place.

This is the moment. This is it. When I knew even silence was able to quiet minds and the voices in our heads. The fact that I didn't have to touch you, just be a few inches away. The song that was playing. All of this. This is the day I fell for the idea that one day I'll love on purpose. I told myself. I want to love on purpose.

There was a moment when my suitcase couldn't fit any more clothes.

I wonder who has my clothes.

I wonder where everything went slowly out of my hand, out of my control.

I can't think anymore.
I can't say, I think…

At this point I am. I am tired once again, but the fault doesn't lie in others this time because my mouth speaks of my mistakes and not someone else's. For we are the creatures that created our minds, even though the world molded them for us. We are the ones who hold the pain of others and choose to run through it like it's our own when we don't have to carry that.

The weight must
be buried this time.

So please don't hold my hand, but just sit beside me. I don't want to cry anymore about how you can't love me because you can barely love yourself, and I won't regret these words when they part my lips and speak. The last time I sat in this place was exactly a year ago. Here I go again, and I might say this time it's different. This time, I want to choose you over my ego. I want to sit here and not take it away because it's cruel to take someone's toys away, right? But why was I a toy to begin with is the real question?

Don't pick up the phone. Don't text me at all. Just don't do it. At one point, I thought you cared and loved me as a person, and that's all I've ever wanted from anyone, even in companionship. But you twisted so many words that they became a sharp knife, and you enjoyed the pressure of it being driven through me.

I would love to tell you, "Leave me alone," but our story doesn't end here.

It ends now.

For someone who doesn't like how this generation shows love, you sure know how to show you're just like them.

And if it was all a lie, then why did you hold my hands like you wanted something

Why did you hold them so close to yours that you asked me so many times not to leave

And still you push and push, and I've met that before because I push people away so easily, like they're disposable

But they're not.

We all matter.

Even me.

I'm sorry I lost my innocence

I'm sorry I lost it along the way

I don't know where I lost it

Maybe it was when a girl kissed me for the first time, because boys were forcing us since we were girls at the time

Maybe it was when my lips were parted inside C building at my high school when I was 15

Or was it on the grass when I would walk around with her

Or was it the parties in senior year when I became some peoples first kiss, and then make out with another, so there was a show for others to watch

When did kissing become sexual for me?

It was intimate without sexual tension or energy before

I wonder if it became something that needed to lead to something else when I was able to be safe in my body and mind

I wonder if the fact that I didn't have to cover myself up anymore while walking down the street so a man wouldn't look at my breasts not even thinking about the fact, I was underage, is carved into me

I wonder if it was the fact that every pair of lips, I tasted knew how to breathe hard and not soft

But why is it that every time my underwear had to come off, I always managed to have a panic attack

It's like I'm a woman all over again

Do I still sexualize the idea based on my freedom as a man?

The contradiction just sits there on my shoulder, unable, I look at the other half of my body as a reminder that as the woman I once was

As her…

Respect her

But I'm not mad at the fact that the reminder is constantly there, I'm so glad

I know how it feels to have someone on top of you as you can't breathe

So, when you feel them soften or their body weaken from fear, you know the word stop without having to ask

Because you were on the other side once too

So, please tell me how they wanted it

Because you knew they didn't, but you still did it anyways

You'll be everything to me

And you will remain everything for as long as I can see you

Even in death, my eyes will stay wide open

I want to hold someone so close that our waists don't need to connect

I want to grab onto a back and feel so deeply that I finally understand

I want to learn what the word love means

I fear that before our bodies would hug, they were never respected

They were grabbed onto
They weren't soft and kind
They were rough and wanting

I hope love finds me and allows me to listen to a voice that finally echoes and teaches me things I haven't thought about before

I hope the words reach my skin to provoke goosebumps

I want to be held, as they don't want anything from me after I kiss their neck once

If poetry and words formed love for me, then I would like nothing more than to express every word I've ever learned

I wish to choose one person and not let go

There will be people who promise me the world, but the world they think I need, not the one I need to be in

You see, a love where you naturally fit into, no need to change to create one

My lips will quietly say your name in elegance, and they will never shout it, for I have tried to love people who needed me to scream their name, and I didn't want to

I will not speak anymore, if it ever leaves my mouth

A compass that comes from vile intentions, if I saw it with no meaning, it would've carved into me and shown me the way to the truth sooner

And the truth is

I don't want to run anymore. I don't want to run away from things that seem way too hard to do. I don't want to let my insecurities and my trauma get the best of me because I feel like if I leave first, then I won't hurt, but the pain comes long after that fact, even if you don't feel it in the moment.

I don't want to run anymore because for the first time, I lay here and tell myself I don't wish to be this person anymore. I don't want to feel ill when I'm tied down and pushed against a corner. It's not real. My lungs contain fresh, clean air. My heart beats red blood and not black liquid anymore. My body has never felt so safe within itself.

So, I won't run anymore.

I will sit with my thoughts every day; this time, I won't let them win. The voices can't trick me anymore. This time I'll fight. This time, I won't let it win ever again.

Please focus on the good once it becomes hard

Allow their hands to touch yours
Allow it to slow your heart rate

Allow the love you hold for others to shower you

Remember that it comes in all forms, and you can't judge the way it comes from others; it's not yours

Reminder: you aren't the same

A reminder that you weren't raised the same

Even if it feels like we were cut from the same cloth, we are not one

We are individuals at the end of the day

You're enough can be for yourself, their enough is different

You're enough
You're enough
You're enough

And I say this not to convince myself but to understand that you are you and I am me and I can't change that

I'm enough.

There are times when we forget we need to be financially stable in this world to survive, and in those moments, you find peace because you're only enjoying life and not paying to live it. To know peace is to know privilege.

If you let people help you,
you realize you're not really alone after all.

I'll happily hold your hand even if you wear the same shirt three times within the same week.

We don’t ask about our favorite things.

The things that come to mind when I’m with my friends are conversations or laughter that can write books and fill stadiums.

"I'm a mess."

You're still worthy of love. Even on your bad days.

Never go to see because I will never be blind to it, for I have felt lost my entire life, yet in a sea of many eyes, I have found a home.

And along the way, you look around and forget how people gravitate towards you and away from you

You look at your friends and see love, so much love

So much happiness

We forget that that's what life is supposed to be

The ones that are kind are around you

They're coming, just wait.

I'm starting to understand why I'm here, what purpose I have

It will pass, right?

The feelings

The love

Everything I hold

It will go away, right?

Or will you keep coming back?

And I'll be the idiot who thinks every time,

It will be different

It's the fact that it's been 6 months, and you cry randomly. You listen to a song a little too long. You miss someone a little too much. You focus on why it happened a little too hard. Then life hits, you realize your reality. The fact that they don't exist anymore… it really hurts. But is it the pain from the longing or is it your guilt because you think you can save everyone?

You can't save anyone.

I don’t enjoy giving up on people but if the push begins getting closer to the cliff and if I fall, what happens if I can’t get up again? At least not this time.

I want to get up.

How many times does your phone have to ring until you pick up the phone.

Please tell me if I mean something.

Please tell me.

Not because I need the validation but maybe the reassurance that I’m wanted here.

Why can’t you understand that.

Why is that so hard?

Proud of me today
Proud of me tomorrow

I only need to hear that I'm proud of myself

I don't need people to tell me that they're proud of me

The thing is
it wouldn't hurt.

I realized I can't make the same mistake my mother did in choosing not to trust anyone

I think it's important to ask for help

Cause when you ask for help

You don't sit in misery waiting ten years for something to happen

In a world where there is community

We all help each other

And it's okay to ask for help

Please ask for help

Please don't remember what it feels like to give up

Even in mixed emotions and hurt ones too
Maybe love can stay even if it's let go

Just remember, only if it's truly wanting to be let go of

Don't give up when things get hard, if you do then it will hurt more when you realize you could've tried your best, you know your best, isn't your worst

My heart doesn't
beat for you,
it beats for me.

Although I hope
it still
skips when
you're nearby…

I know things change, but I want to feel cared about again

Truly cared about, truly enough

I want to feel it like I did the first time we knew that things weren't so easy

I still sleep at the edge of my king-sized
bed because sometimes it feels like I'm
waiting for someone to fill that space

And then I move to the middle

I don't want to have sex with other people to fill the missing pieces you couldn't provide.

The art of:
letting go.

It will always cost you.

People will always be enough for me.

But I'm not going to fight someone against themselves every day to figure out if I'm worth their time.

Look in the mirror, then show me how you feel.

You were never a waste of time

I'm just not good with words
some...

times

The only regret I'll ever finally come across will not be because of someone's existence in my life, but of the loneliness of not trying hard enough. The ache of not shedding skin to meet those at the level you can translate well. I'll regret not fighting for you. That's the day I'll finally regret something.

Give me what you can, and that will always be enough; they are the only kind words we want to receive daily.

The familiarities that you're used to when being strung in a long-term relationship, my ideology of being with someone is still modified like I have to be in that exact same relationship in order to calm my nervous system down. In conclusion, I'm not ready for anything at all. How do I expect stability without questioning myself first?

Give me what you can. Some of us have buckets of water, a few of us have only droplets, it's not fair to shove our privilege into their faces.

I've honestly never wanted to be in a committed relationship. That's why I would go to different people all the time when I was younger. I'm a very miserable person when I have a committed partner.

And I'm still battling myself with the idea that I have to have a stable partner when that's not something I want, if I wanted that I would've stayed, I would've made it work.

I'm boyfriend material but I think I'm boyfriend material to show people what they deserve not to be what they deserve and I'm okay with that.

Don't build houses with me

Maybe I'll get bored one day and leave you in it…

I only leave those that never felt like home, like there was no effort, there was no time put into it, and heart. I can't stay in a house only built on my ideas, that's not fair, that's not love.

If you didn't want this, you wouldn't be sitting here at 5 am, wasting sleep, to finally feel whole.

A finished painting.

I don't think the worst pain is when someone doesn't love you back

It's when they do

But they're so scared that they never even try

And life is too short not to try

I fear one day I'll find a love so deep; I'll find them in every universe, and if I continue to get it wrong, I will continue living until I find them in the right one.

Sometimes treasure
is meant to be
found, not meant to
be kept.

I think the best way I can describe it is when you're sitting in front of an art piece, and you look at it.

You can't touch it, you can feel it, you can admire it, listen, it will tell you all it's been through, but you can't buy it just because you want to. It's hard to get. It deserves more than that. It's priceless.

But if you learn to enjoy the moment that you're in, its presence, and learn to let go, you'll enjoy every single minute of it.

That's how I love.

I'm patient, I listen, I admire.

Detach.

I let go.

We don't bleed the same

I want to pretend and tell you that your blood type can save me

But that's not how it works; you're different, and the ones who bleed the same can heal together in many other ways

I'll go through
my phases just to
meet you.

Sit down inside your head and have a conversation with yourself.

For everything that you need and will ever want is inside you already.

The mirrors we try to turn to others are a facade waiting to be discovered.

The brightest minds will hold darkness in, like it's their birthright.

The quiet anchor on the sea floor is still drowning.

You have the power to pick it up.

Don't forget to pick it up.

I belonged to you the minute I stepped through a door and saw you sitting on the couch in all black.

I'll sit here with a projector behind me replaying your laugh, and I'll cry my eyes out at the thought that I can't create new ones with you

I can't turn back time

I'll be in a trance of heroine, only I know about

Sitting in silence with my drool coming out of my mouth and the snot dripping out of my nose

Like I'm dying and my body is rejecting everything I've ever felt was real in this world

I can feel my body collapsing, and every vein, irritated

My mind and body are against me

The pain is unbearable

I can't wish this on anyone

I didn't know bumping heads was so aggressive for some.

Aren't we supposed to be learning from one another?

I've only ever bumped heads with people who truly don't know themselves.

If I show love, I don't care what hate comes towards me.

I'll always choose love; my heart will be pure while yours rots.

This is how I know I'm not important to you

You're only wanting me when it's needed for you

My picture frame stays behind your door, while everyone else has hung theirs up proudly amongst their things

I'm not one to hold a grudge, but I think this one's worth judging

These poems bleed about the love I have within me

It was all in my head

Every single thing

To no one but a feeling, it was only a feeling.

Made in the USA
Coppell, TX
17 February 2026